I0503523

From the Author of "The Magic of Thinking Big: Manifesting Your Dreams

HOW

Effective Tools

TO BUILD

That Are Scientifically Proven

YOUR

To Help You Become

SELF

More Confident

ESTEEM

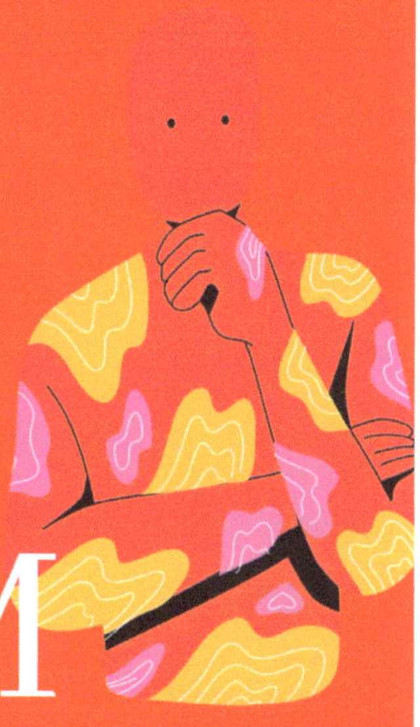

BY VALENTO THOMAS

How to Build Your Self-Esteem and Love What You See in the Mirror.

In today's fast-paced world, self-esteem and self-love are crucial for a fulfilling and happy life. Building self-esteem isn't just about feeling good momentarily; it's about creating a foundation that allows you to thrive, be resilient, and love what you see in the mirror every day. Here's a comprehensive guide to help you on this journey.

1. Understand Self-Esteem

Self-esteem is your overall sense of self-worth or personal value. It's about how much you appreciate and like yourself regardless of the circumstances. High self-esteem is a key to mental well-being and a positive outlook on life.

2. Identify and Challenge Negative Beliefs

The first step to building self-esteem is to identify and challenge your negative beliefs. These are often deeply rooted and can stem from past experiences, societal expectations, or critical self-talk. Write down these negative thoughts and analyze them. Are they based on facts or just perceptions? Replace them with positive affirmations and truths about yourself.

3. Set Realistic Goals

Setting and achieving realistic goals can greatly enhance your self-esteem. Break down your goals into manageable steps and celebrate your achievements along the way. This will help you see your progress and build confidence.

4. Practice Self-Care

Taking care of your physical, emotional, and mental well-being is essential. Exercise regularly, eat healthily, get enough sleep, and engage in activities that bring you joy. When you take care of your body, it reflects in your mind and boosts your self-esteem.

5. Surround Yourself with Positive People

The people around you have a significant impact on how you feel about yourself. Surround yourself with positive, supportive individuals who uplift you and encourage you. Limit your interactions with those who bring negativity into your life.

6. Accept Your Flaws and Celebrate Your Strengths

Nobody is perfect. Accept your flaws and understand that they make you unique. At the same time, recognize and celebrate your strengths. Make a list of your achievements and the qualities you admire in yourself.

7. Practice Gratitude

Gratitude can shift your focus from what's lacking in your life to what you already have. Each day, take a moment to reflect on what you are grateful for. This practice can increase your overall happiness and appreciation for yourself.

8. Develop a Positive Body Image

Loving what you see in the mirror starts with developing a positive body image. Focus on what your body can do rather than how it looks. Dress in a way that makes you feel good and confident. Avoid comparing yourself to others, especially on social media, where images are often altered and unrealistic.

9. Engage in Activities You Enjoy

Doing things you love can significantly boost your self-esteem. Whether it's a hobby, a sport, or a creative endeavor, engaging in activities that bring you joy can enhance your sense of accomplishment and self-worth.

10. Seek Professional Help if Needed

Sometimes, building self-esteem requires professional guidance. If you find it challenging to improve your self-esteem on your own, consider seeking help from a therapist or counselor. They can provide you with tools and techniques tailored to your needs.

CONCLUSION

BUILDING SELF-ESTEEM AND LOVING WHAT YOU SEE IN THE MIRROR IS A JOURNEY THAT REQUIRES TIME, EFFORT, AND PATIENCE. BY UNDERSTANDING SELF-ESTEEM, CHALLENGING NEGATIVE BELIEFS, SETTING REALISTIC GOALS, PRACTICING SELF-CARE, SURROUNDING YOURSELF WITH POSITIVITY, ACCEPTING YOUR FLAWS, PRACTICING GRATITUDE, DEVELOPING A POSITIVE BODY IMAGE, ENGAGING IN ENJOYABLE ACTIVITIES, AND SEEKING PROFESSIONAL HELP IF NEEDED, YOU CAN CREATE A SOLID FOUNDATION FOR A HEALTHIER, HAPPIER, AND MORE CONFIDENT YOU. EMBRACE THE JOURNEY AND REMEMBER THAT YOU ARE WORTH IT.

11. Practice Mindfulness and Meditation

Mindfulness and meditation can help you stay present and aware of your thoughts and feelings without judgment. This practice can reduce stress, increase self-awareness, and help you develop a compassionate and non-critical view of yourself. Incorporate mindfulness exercises or meditation into your daily routine, even if it's just for a few minute11. Practice Mindfulness and Meditation

Mindfulness and meditation can help you stay present and aware of your thoughts and feelings without judgment. This practice can reduce stress, increase self-awareness, and help you develop a compassionate and non-critical view of yourself. Incorporate mindfulness exercises or meditation into your daily routine, even if it's just for a few minutes.s.

12. Develop Healthy Boundaries

Learning to say no and setting boundaries is crucial for maintaining self-respect and self-esteem. Recognize your limits and communicate them clearly to others. This will help you avoid burnout and ensure that you are treated with the respect you deserve.

13. Reflect on Your Values and Beliefs

Understanding your core values and beliefs can guide your actions and decisions, helping you live authentically and with purpose. Reflect on what truly matters to you and ensure that your life aligns with these values. Living in harmony with your beliefs can boost your self-esteem and self-worth.

14. Engage in Positive Self-Talk

Replace self-criticism with positive self-talk. Encourage and affirm yourself just as you would a close friend. When you catch yourself thinking negatively, pause and reframe your thoughts in a more positive and supportive light.

15. Keep a Journal

Journaling can be a powerful tool for self-discovery and reflection. Write about your thoughts, feelings, and experiences. This practice can help you process emotions, identify patterns, and celebrate your progress. It's a safe space to explore your inner world and reinforce positive self-image.

16. Take Responsibility for Your Actions

Taking responsibility for your actions, both good and bad, empowers you to make changes and grow. Acknowledge your mistakes without dwelling on them, and focus on what you can learn and how you can improve. This approach fosters resilience and self-respect.

17. Volunteer and Help Others

Helping others can give you a sense of purpose and boost your self-esteem. Volunteering your time and skills not only benefits others but also provides you with a sense of accomplishment and connection. It reminds you of your ability to make a positive impact in the world

18. Celebrate Small Wins

Don't wait for major milestones to celebrate your achievements. Recognize and celebrate small wins along the way. This practice reinforces your progress and helps you stay motivated. Every step forward, no matter how small, is a step toward greater self-esteem and self-love.

19. Visualize Your Success

Visualization is a powerful tool for building confidence and self-esteem. Take time to imagine yourself achieving your goals and living your best life. Visualize the steps you'll take and the positive outcomes you'll experience. This mental rehearsal can increase your belief in your abilities and motivate you to take action.

20. Practice Patience and Self-Compassion

Building self-esteem and self-love is a gradual process. Be patient with yourself and understand that there will be ups and downs. Practice self-compassion by treating yourself with kindness and understanding, especially during challenging times. Remember that growth takes time, and it's okay to progress at your own pace.

Embrace the Journey

The journey to building self-esteem and loving what you see in the mirror is deeply personal and unique to each individual. Embrace the process with an open heart and mind. Celebrate your uniqueness and the progress you make along the way. By implementing these strategies, you can cultivate a healthy sense of self-worth and a positive self-image, leading to a more fulfilling and joyful life.

VALENTO THOMAS

THINK OUTSIDE THE BOX

A book on being 'creative'
and how to actually be one.

NEXT BOOK